EASY AS ABC

Warren Rylands and Samantha Nugent

LET'S READ
AV²
BY WEIGL™
ADDED VALUE • AUDIO VISUAL

AV² provides enriched content that supplements and complements this book. Weigl's AV² books strive to create inspired learning and engage young minds in a total learning experience.

Your AV² Media Enhanced books come alive with...

Audio
Listen to sections of the book read aloud.

Go to **www.av2books.com**, and enter this book's unique code.

Key Words
Study vocabulary, and complete a matching word activity.

BOOK CODE

Y235733

Video
Watch informative video clips.

Quizzes
Test your knowledge.

AV² by Weigl brings you media enhanced books that support active learning.

Embedded Weblinks
Gain additional information for research.

Slide Show
View images and captions, and prepare a presentation.

Try This!
Complete activities and hands-on experiments.

... and much, much more!

Published by AV² by Weigl
350 5th Avenue, 59th Floor
New York, NY 10118

Website: www.av2books.com

Library of Congress Control Number: 2015940619

ISBN 978-1-4896-3525-9 (hardcover)
ISBN 978-1-4896-3527-3 (single user eBook)
ISBN 978-1-4896-3528-0 (multi-user eBook)

Printed in the United States of America in Brainerd, Minnesota
1 2 3 4 5 6 7 8 9 0 19 18 17 16 15

052015
WEP050815

Project Coordinator: Katie Gillespie   Art Director: Terry Paulhus

Weigl acknowledges Getty Images and iStock as the primary image suppliers for this title.

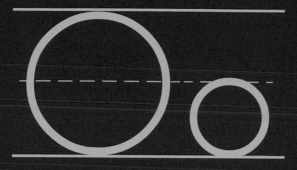

CONTENTS

2   AV² Book Code

4   Discovering the Letter O

6   Starting Words with O

8   O Inside a Word

10   Ending Words with O

12   Learning O Names

14   Different O Sounds

16   Long O Sounds

18   Short O Sounds

20   Having Fun with O

22   O and the Alphabet

24   Log on to www.av2books.com

Let's explore the letter

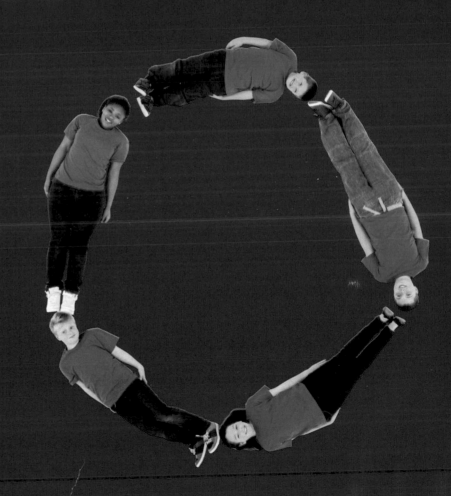

The uppercase letter 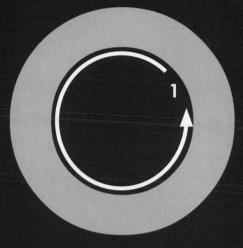 looks like this

The lowercase letter O looks like this

The letter O can start many words.

owl

ocean

oven

orange

onion

7

The letter O can be inside a word.

wag_o_n

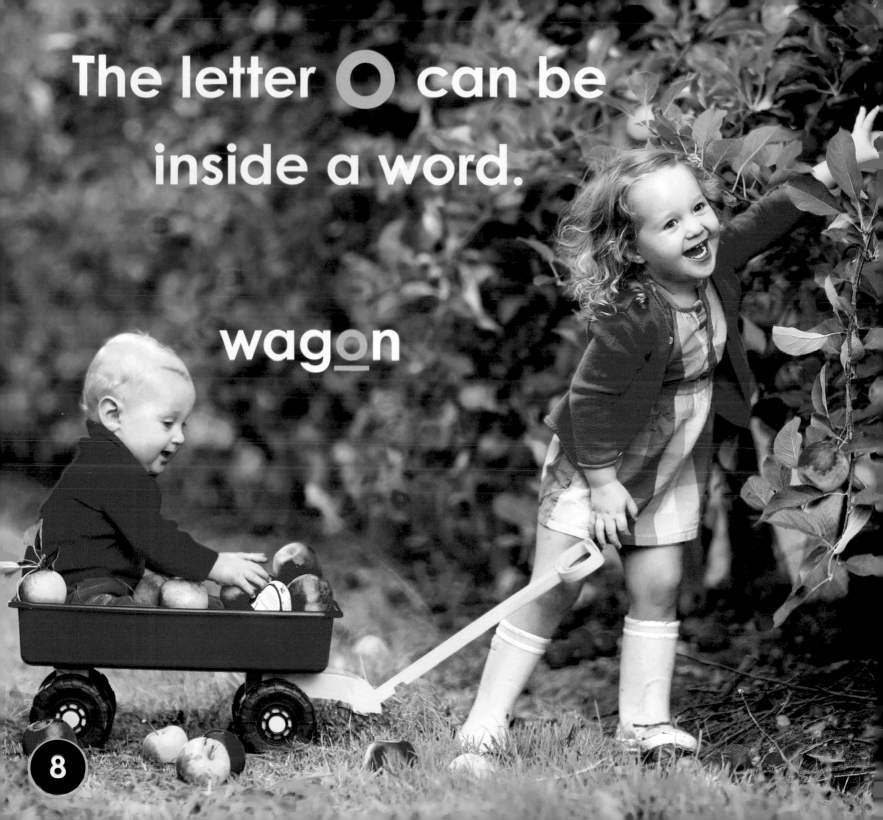

brown

crown

dog

stop

9

The letter O can be at the end of a word.

volcano

buffalo

yoyo

taco

gecko

11

Many names start with an uppercase O.

Olga

Owen can find anything.

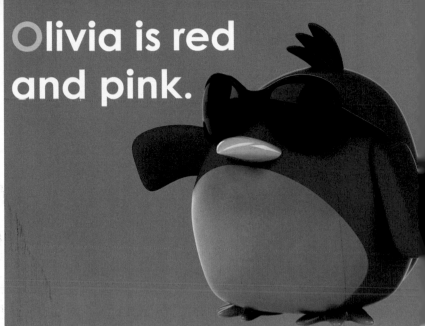

Olivia is red and pink.

Oliver can skate.

Oscar is tall.

13

The letter O makes different sounds.

home

pot

The word hōme  has a long ō sound.

 The word pŏt has a short ŏ sound.

Some words have
a long Ō sound.

ōwn

clōse

almōst

bōth

thōse

17

Other words have

a short ŏ sound.

gŏt

ŏff

tŏp

nŏt

lŏng

Having Fun with O

The old owls stopped by the ocean. Octopus Olga was cooking tacos and cookies.

The old owls took the cookies and tacos. They loaded their wagon with the food.

On their way out, they found a yoyo. It was an orange and brown yoyo.

Oh, what an October that was!

The alphabet has **26** letters.

O is the fifteenth letter in the alphabet.

Aa Bb Cc Dd Ee

Ff Gg Hh Ii Jj Kk

Ll Mm Nn Oo Pp

Qq Rr Ss Tt Uu Vv

Ww Xx Yy Zz

23

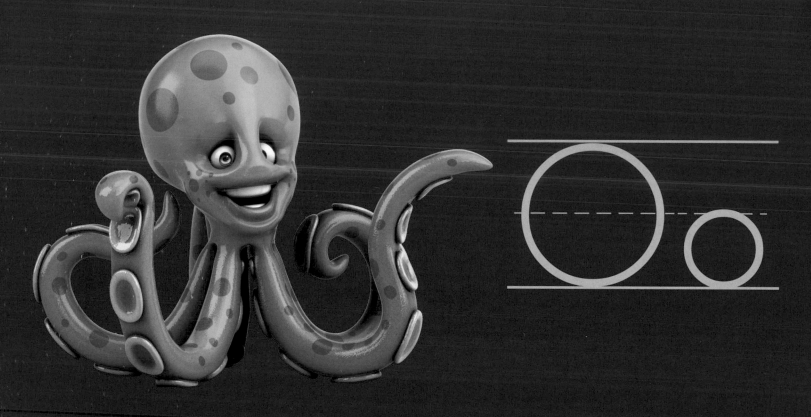